On pages 8-9,
an air view of Ostia Antica.

In the enclosed insert,
the general map with captions.

Relief with an orator, scribes, and listeners

A. PASCOLINI

# INDEX

© 1979 Editore Armando Armando

1990 Prima ristampa

© Armando Armando s.r.l.
Piazza Sidney Sonnino 13 - Roma

21-08-006

ISBN 88-7144-153-2

Traslation by Linda Kroeger Pascolini

# Aldo Pascolini

# OSTIA

**ARMANDO
EDITORE**

FIUME TEVERE

MUSEO

ANTICO LITORALE

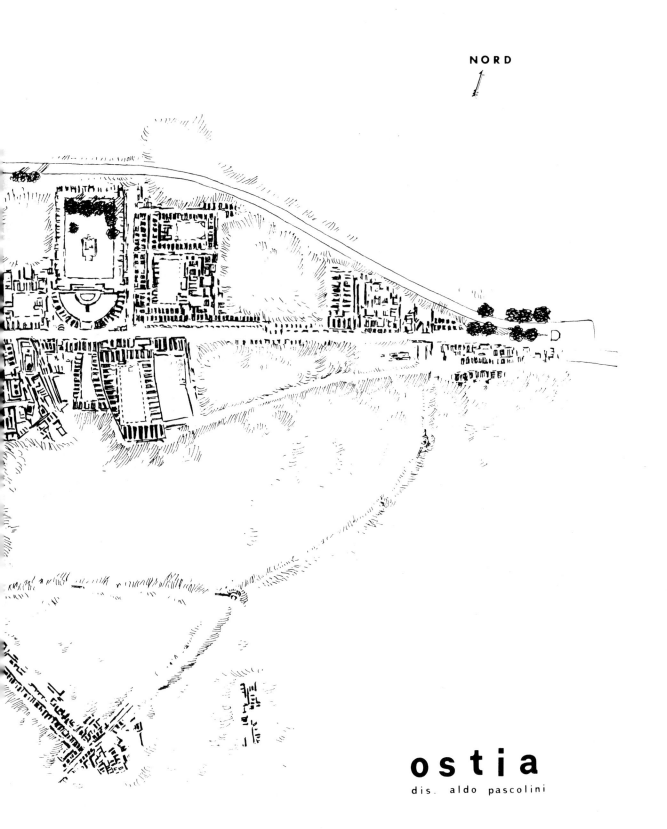

NORD

ostia
dis. aldo pascolini

# PREFACE

It is of a recent event last May that this work written with such enthusiasm and clear simplicity by Aldo Pascolini, long-time collaborator of young scholars and archaeologists of Ostia, has made me think: the presence in Ostia for an entire day of a thousand French children, chosen from among the most deserving in the junior secondary schools of Paris.

From the sun's earliest light until its last ray, these children lived among Ostia's walls, following the ancient streets, stopping by taverns and fountains, eating their lunch inside of the houses, reading extracts from Latin authors in the theater, bringing back to light facts and personages from the history of Rome. The goal that the teachers had set for themselves had been fully reached: within the brief but complete span of a day, the children had become part of the reality of the daily life of an ancient city, they had touched and breathed that atmosphere of authentic Roman civilization, genuine in its structures, pure in its horizons, which Ostia still preserves, miraculously, wonderfully, between the ribbon of the Tiber and the pleasant Roman countryside bordering the ancient sea coast. I am certain that they will never forget the experience lived among the old stones which in turn had recovered, by merit of these young people, an extraordinary magic of sounds and colors, regaining function and prestige now that they had been vivified by

a deep act of love. For a year, in fact, the young students had dedicated themselves to Ostia's history and monuments so that reaching them and recognizing them was all one.

And this is the purpose that the book can achieve: prepare those who read it, children or not, to better know so that they might be able to better love our antiquity, appreciating that which it can also offer to modern man: richer of means and knowledge, better prepared and disenchanted, and for this very reason perhaps partly impoverished of that extraordinary instrument of richness which is the imagination; but it is nevertheless still man himself in front of the fundamental themes of his humanity.

★

Ostia Antica, so distant and alien from the modern Ostia Lido born on the silting of that sea which once lapped its houses along the Severian Way where now the Via della Scafa leads to Fiumicino, so discreet and reserved in the green oasis that surrounds it compared to the nearby industrial and commercial areas, represents perhaps the most complete example of a Roman city of the Imperial epoch.

It is not grandiose like its contemporary sister cities in Africa, it is not scenographic and sumptuous like the metropolises of Asia Minor or Syria, but it keeps a human proportion in all of its aspects, from city planning to building, from artistic expressions to religious manifestations.

It is with reason, therefore, that we should see reflected in Ostia the image in miniature of Rome which a far-seeing plan of expropriation carried out by archaeologists between 1930 and 1938 has protected time-wise and space-wise so that it might remain a field of study and meditation for future generations.

Ostia, November 10, 1978

VALNEA SANTA MARIA SCRINARI
*Superintendent of Antiquities at Ostia*

# BIRTH, DEVELOPMENT AND END OF OSTIA

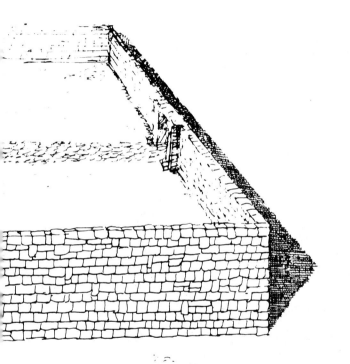

*THE CASTRUM OF ANCUS MARTIUS AND ITS RESTORATIONS*

From the Latin *ostium* (river mouth) the city of Ostia took its name.

According to texts come down to us from Ennius, writer and poet living around the second century B.C., from the historian Titus Livy, from the writer and orator Cicero, from the historians Aurelius Victor, governor of Pannonia at the time of Theodosius, and Eutropius who lived in the fourth century A.D., to mention only a few scholars of Roman civilization, Ostia was founded around the sixth century B.C. by Ancus Martius, fourth king of Rome, as in the legend. The king wanted to assure an outlet for the military and commercial expansion of the then small Rome. After conquering

Mural structure of the « Castrum » (detail)

the coastal populations in the way of this project, Ancus Martius had a *castrum* (fortified citadel) built near the mouth of the river for a garrison of soldiers to defend navigation on the Tiber and detached sentinels up and down the sea coast.

But the *castrum* which is still clearly discernible among its ruins is almost certainly a remaking of the old *castrum* of Ancus Martius.

### FROM FORTIFIED CITADEL TO MILITARY AND COMMERCIAL HARBOR

Ostia, then, was the first colony of the Roman expansion. Of the Royal period, very little has come to surface during excavations of the city, but we must suppose that the fortified citadel changed its original aspect very soon because of the considerable building expansion. Once that their conquest had been consolidated, the Romans then made Ostia their military port and commercial base, linked to Rome by the fluvial route of the Tiber.

Certainly, it is in the Republican period that the city had its first expansion. Republican constructions were built outside of the *castrum's* walls, too limiting by then for the needs of a rising harbor city, and consequently the quality itself of life changed considerably. The Temple of Hercules and the two small temples nearby were erected; the four small temples on the Decumanus Maximus also should be from the same period.

### THE FIRST HORREA

The first enormous *horrea* (warehouses) were then erected for storing the wares that arrived from overseas. Houses were built along the Decumanus Maximus and

14

the Cardi Maximi which were extensions outside of the *castrum* of its old streets.

The city grew and prospered at an equal pace with Rome. Cicero reminds us that in 267 B.C. four *Quaestores* of the fleet were created with naval and costal surveillance duties. One was assigned to Ostia, and the city, besides having the characteristic of fortress and safeguard of the Tiber, also had to answer the needs of a port and maritime city and hence to provide for the storage of goods destined for Rome and vice versa.

During the war against Hannibal, Ostia obtained for its men, together with those of Anzio, the privilege of exemption from military service in the fighting legions so that they could defend these two very important ports of Rome.

### DESTRUCTIVE LIGHTNING AND PLUNDER

In 208 B.C., the city walls and a gate of the citadel were hit by lightning. And it's still Livy who gives us more news regarding destructive lightning. In 199 B.C., the citizens of Ostia announced to the Senate of Rome that their Temple of Jupiter had been struck by lightning.

In 87 B.C., during the civil war between Marius and Sulla, Marius succeeded in taking possession of the colony which was laid to sacking and devastation by his soldiers. Many maintain that Ostia sided with Sulla, so that afterwards he repaid it by enclosing it with great walls.

### SHIP YARDS AND NEW BUILDINGS

Ostia very soon acquired a notable role and importance for Rome and emerged for its great mercantile and military traffic, due also to its geographical position which made it the first port of Rome. Ship yards arose in which were built both light warships with several levels of oars or large cargo ships with sails and small barges which served for transportation by animal haulage (towing) along the Tiber's embankments up to Rome.

Merchants and maritime contractors settled in this city, enrichening it with their commerce and building stupendous *domus* (homes) there. Provisions employees in charge of controlling merchandise settled in apartment houses, thus facilitating the rise of a new intermediate class between the patrician and the plebeian. Shopkeepers and small traders completed the lymph which fed this city.

Reconstruction of a work scene

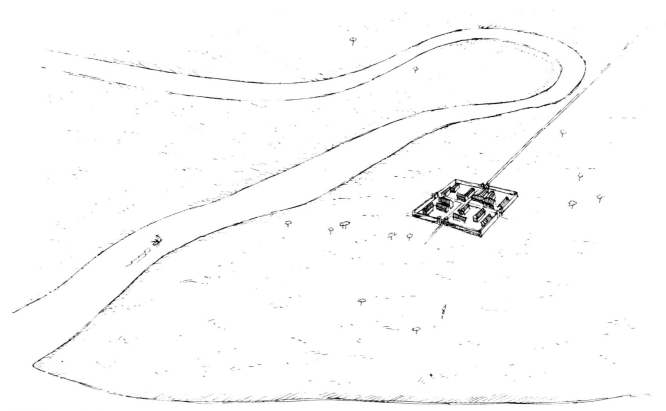

IV Century B.C. (ca.) « Castrum »

II Century B.C. (ca.)

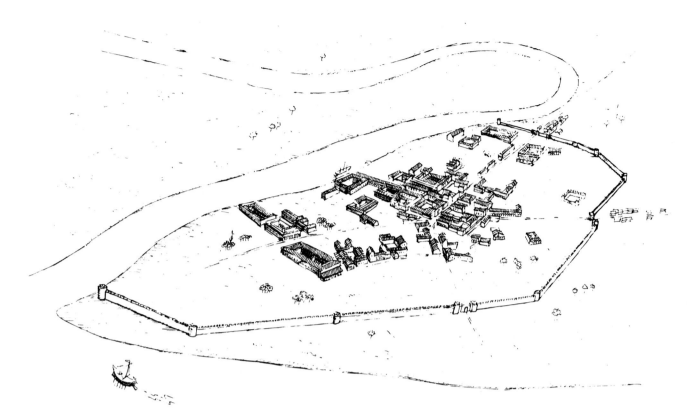

I Century B.C. (with the co-called Sullan Wall)

After the III Century A.D.

## THEATER, TEMPLES, PUBLIC BUILDINGS AND RESTORATIONS

Under one of Agrippa's consulates, in 12 B.C., the theater was built. Temples and public buildings arose and old buildings were restored. The magistrate P. Lucilius Gamala, very generous patron of Ostia, restored the Temple of Vulcan and repaired the temples of Venus and Ceres and paved a stretch of the Decumanus Maximus at his own expense. During the Augustan age, various buildings arose toward the city's outskirts.

The first two centuries of Empire resulted the most flourishing and productive for Ostia. State administrative offices took up the city's central buildings. The emperor Claudius, who greatly loved Ostia, it seems, often took part personally in the religious and social life of this city. He placed a detachment of guards in Ostia to be in charge of fire protection, public security, and traffic control. After the probable silting up of the fluvial port on the Tiber, Claudius built a new port for Ostia about two miles northwest, digging it inland along the coast.

## HEXAGONAL DOCK, DRINKING WATER AND LAND RECLAMATION

The emperor Trajan built a harbor in 104 A.D., a very beautiful hexagonal internal dock with new wharves and an ample canal. The emperor Caligula gave Ostia a lead pipeline which distributed drinking water to the city. The emperor Nero, using the rubble from Rome's Great Fire, reclaimed some swamp areas inland from Ostia.

18

spices, everything was crowded orderly into those rooms. Precious woods, leathers, cloth, ivory, artifacts from other provinces, even delicate and frivolous perfumes from Egypt, before reaching the Roman matrons, left their exotic trace in Ostia. The beautiful Greek and Egyptian marble roughly hewed in the quarries into the forms requested of the quarriers by the Roman architects first came through Ostia from where they were later taken in order to reach and beautify the *domus*, the temples, or other public build-

Large « horrea »

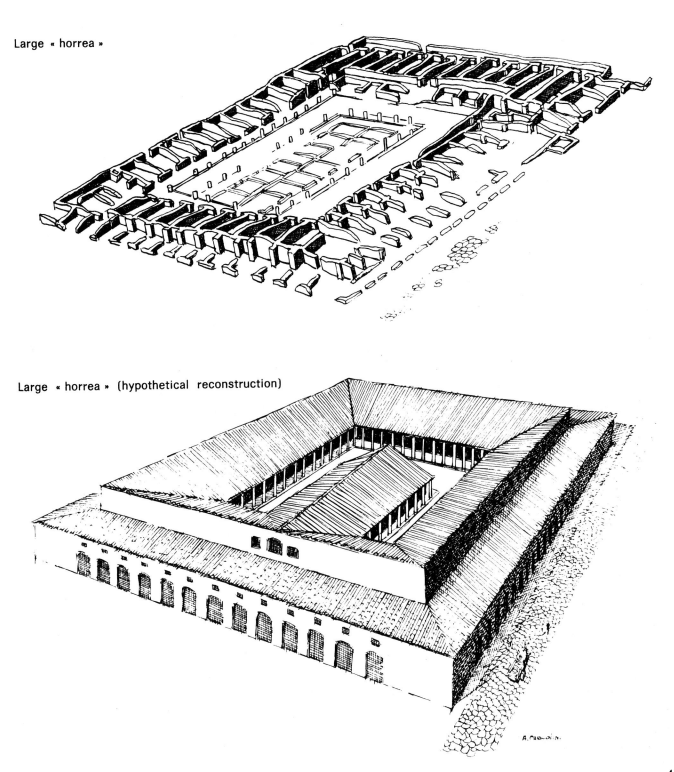

Large « horrea » (hypothetical reconstruction)

43

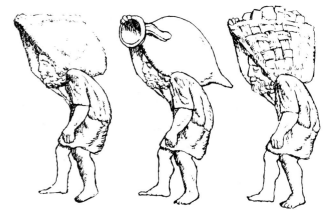

Funeral reliefs from the III Century A.D.

44

Vat storehouse

ings. One of these loads, after having laboriously faced the dangers of navigation on the Mediterranean and at last safe in Ostia's haven, sank by some strange mishap during the initial phase of river transport toward Rome. That accident, which happened centuries ago, has allowed us, however, to recover from the Tiber a series of blocks of quarried marble completely preserved by the river's muddy sands. Columns, bases, thin slabs in stupendous polychrome marble, barely shaped in their essential forms and ready for the finishing touches, are now grouped alongside the inside parking lot of the ruins, ready for the visitor's admiration.

*DOCUMENTED WELL-BEING OF A PRIVILEGED COLONY*

So Ostia, Rome's emporium city, accumulates wares and wealth. Naturally, to benefit from this situation are its inhabitants, also, who enjoy particular advantages and comforts compared to other Roman colonies. This well-being shows through in the greater part of Ostia's buildings, witnessing to a refinement and luxury rarely found in other Roman cities. That Ostia must have enjoyed a certain well-being is born witness

to in an historical source which remembers Nero who asked the (well-off) inhabitants of Ostia for furniture to furnish the shelters where refugees from Rome's Great Fire could live temporarily.

THE HORREA OF GREATEST INTEREST *:

71.  The Epagathian Horrea
72.  The Small Market
78.  The Apartment Building of the Vats
91.  The Large Horrea
112.  The Horrea of Hortensius

* The numbers correspond to those on the general map.

# THE THEATER

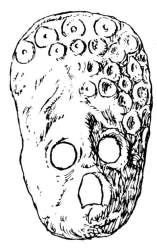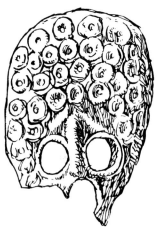

Theatrical masks

The theater was an imposing structure; it was built in 12 A.D. by the consul Agrippa. Restored more than once in ancient times and then enlarged, it could hold, comfortably seated, over three thousand five hundred spectators. The *cavea* with its tiers of seats was divided into sectors, the first rows being reserved for authorities.

The semicircular space called orchestra at the foot of the seating area was reserved for sacred ceremonies. The stage had a permanent scenery decorated with three doors

46

A. PASCOLINI

Circus scene (marble tablet)

47

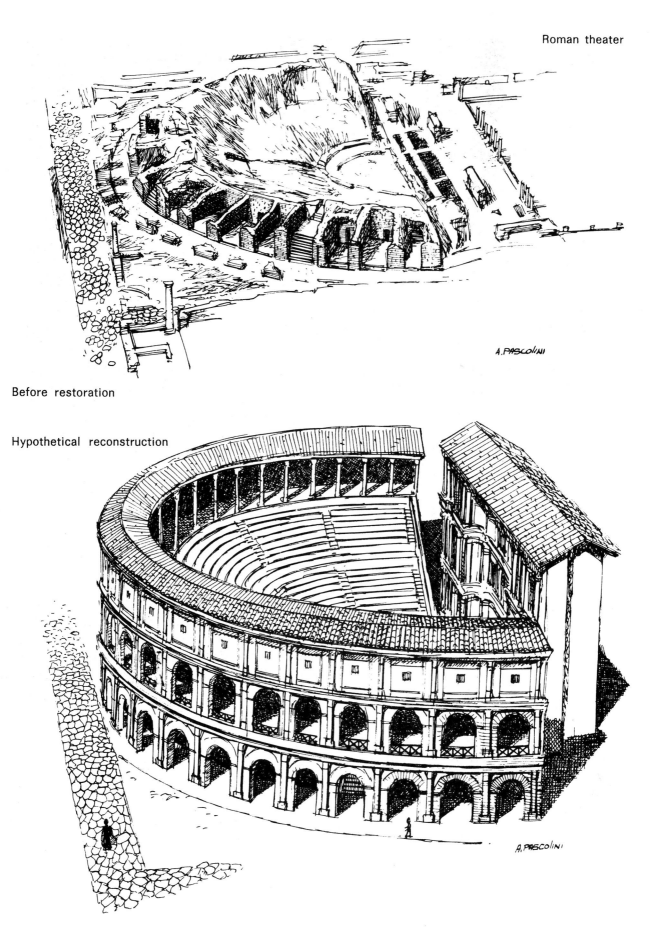

Roman theater

Before restoration

Hypothetical reconstruction

A. PASCOLINI

A. PASCOLINI

48

A. PASCOLINI

from which the actors entered and one several stories high decorated with niches having columns at each side.

In antiquity, theater people were almost always men and consequently they had to recite in female roles as well. That did not create particular difficulties in that they used masks to cover their faces anyway. Generally, these masks represented joy or sadness and the actors changed them according to that which they wanted to express.

Performances were usually comedies, tragedies, or mimed dances. Two large cisterns underneath the seating area make it presumable that shows with water displays were also given.

But still other amusements and shows delighted the ancient inhabitants of Ostia. Although it has not been brought to light yet, Ostia also must have had a circus where it was possible to follow wild chariot races or gladiator fights or sham hunts with exotic animals (*venationes*). On the gods' and patrons' festivals, and in Ostia there must have been many of them, occasions were not lacking for spending an enjoyable day. The arrival of a fleet or the visit of an emperor added other motives for diversion.

Many men, then, ended their evenings in a tavern in front of a jug of good wine between some good talk and a game of dice, probably to the vexation of many matrons forced to run after their spouses from one tavern to another.

49

# THE CORPORATIONS

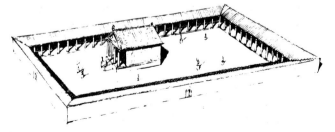

Corporations' Forum (hypothetical reconstruction)

The Corporations' Forum was the vital center of the great Roman maritime trade. Here, all of the commercial agencies from other provinces that had trade relations with Rome were gathered. In the more than sixty offices that lined the forum, samples probably were displayed of those products that the traders then dealt with in large stocks. African and Spanish and Alexandrian traders, importers and exporters of valuable woods, cordage, cereals, oils, and wines are still well characterized by ships, names, and products in the portico's mosaics.

View of the Theater and of the Corporations' Forum

# THE HARBOR

Scene of loading or unloading in the port (detail from a Corporation mosaic)

A. PASCOLINI

## FOOD SUPPLY STRUCTURES AND SHIP YARDS

Legend tells that Aeneas landed at the mouth of the Tiber where the port of Ostia later arose. Ostia's harbor structures have not been found. The Tiber, changing course, perhaps has carried them away definitely or else still hides them in its turbid sands. We do know, however, that Ostia had a fluvial port and that during the first phase of

52

Coin with the port of Ostia

Ostia's lighthouse (from the mosaic in the Baths of the Lighthouse)

Oxen towing a barge of wares along the Tiber from Ostia to Rome

its life it served Rome's commercial and military growth well enough.

*MARITIME TRAFFIC WITH HUNDREDS OF SHIPS UP TO 400 OARS*

Many ancient historians have recorded from time to time facts regarding the maritime traffic at Ostia, but without giving very many details. For example, in 267 B.C., as Cicero reminds us, with the institution of the *Quaestores,* Ostia took up the aspect of a port city and emporium as well as that which it already had as a fortified city for the defense of the Tiber. Livy recalls that in 217 B.C., cargo ships having set sail from Ostia were bringing food supplies to the Roman army in Spain engaged in fighting the First Punic War, but were captured by the Carthaginian fleet so that a consul was

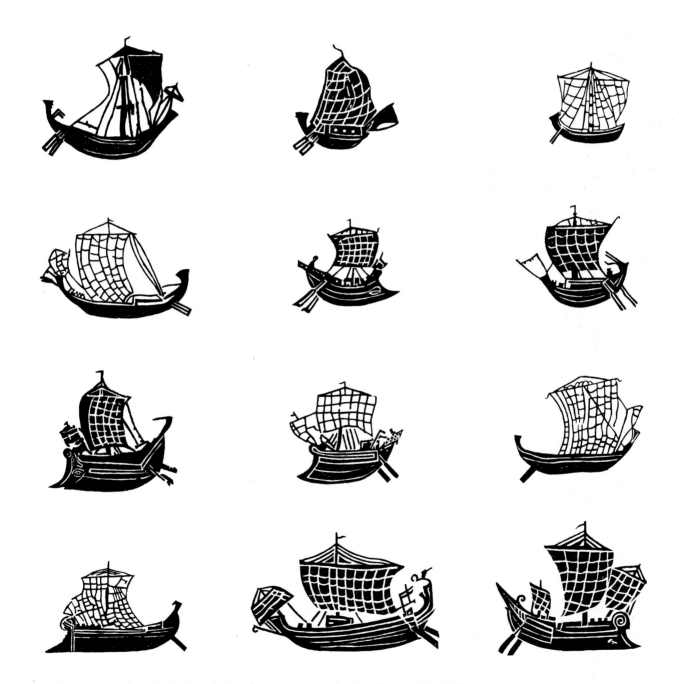

Types of cargo (mercantile) ships taken from mosaics in the Corporations' Forum

ordered to go from Rome to Ostia to recuperate all of the ships possible and be able to follow the enemy fleet. In 216 B.C., the fleet of Gerone of Syracuse landed at Ostia with approximately 162 ships. In 212 B.C., the grain from Sardinia was gathered in Ostia. In 211 B.C., it's still Livy who reminds us about it, P. Cornelius Scipio set sail from Ostia for Spain with thirty *quinqueremi* (ships with five levels of oars). In 208 B.C., there were thirty ships in Ostia for repairs. That demonstrates that there already existed in Ostia at that time ship yards so well equipped as to be able to handle such a great work load.

In 204 B.C., the ship carrying the simulacrum of the goddess Cybele arrived in Ostia, causing great rejoicing among its inhabitants. In 67 B.C., a squadron of ships which had been gathered in Ostia for the purpose of putting down the Cilician pirates were by these very pirates assaulted and destroyed so that Cicero lashed out against the carelessness and the irresponsibility of the

one who had been in charge of this operation. Pliny narrates that in 40 A.D. Rome was in possession of a new type of *quinqueremi* with the incredible number of four hundred oars.

### CLAUDIUS'S NEW PORT FOR LARGE CARGO SHIPS

As time went on, however, something must have changed: either the port's structures were no longer fit for the new, large merchant ships or else, as is more likely, the Tiber had completely silted up the harbor zone at its mouth, making it almost impracticable.

The emperor Claudius, with an incredible financial effort, created a new port about two miles northwest of Ostia, having it excavated entirely inland along the coast. The harbor which took his name (Claudius's Port) was then inaugurated by Nero in 55 A.D. In spite of the imposing harbor facilities (still visible in the area of the Leo-

nardo da Vinci International Airport), it had a brief lifespan. According to Tacitus, it was damaged by a tremendous gale in which two hundred ships that were harbored there for loading and unloading their cargoes were sunk and in which another hundred ships that had taken refuge in the Tiber were destroyed by a colossal fire which broke out as a result of the storm.

## HEXAGONAL DOCK AND TRAJAN'S CANAL

In 104 A.D., as a complement to Claudius's vast harbor basin, the emperor Trajan built an internal dock in hexagonal form which was connected to the old port structures by new elements of completion. He also had a canal dug between the Tiber and the sea (the Trajan *Fovea*) which permitted the renewal of river navigation to Rome, impeded up until then by continuous silting up of the river's mouth.

In 430 A.D., Rutilius Namatianus, a Roman historian, described Ostia's port situation thus: the river's right arm had dried up and the left one was inaccessible to ships due to the excessive sand that filled the river's mouth. He concluded by saying that of Aeneas's ancient site only its glory remained.

## SILTING AND THE USE OF BARGES FOR TOWING GOODS

In the sixth century after Christ, the Greek historian Procopius described the procedure for unloading goods. When traders arrived in port with their ships, they unloaded their wares and then reloaded them onto some barges which had long ropes tied between them and the necks of oxen. The latter, following the Tiber's bank, towed the barges as though they were carts.

In the ninth century after Christ, river navigation was reduced to Ostia's arm alone, now called the «Fiumara». This is cited in the maritime treaty made between Romans and Genoese in 1166 for the free navigation in their respective ports.

# THE SHOPS AND TRADES

Poultry vendor (marble tablet)

Butcher shop (marble tablet)

## BUILDING STRUCTURE OF SHOPS

Retail stores occupied the ground floor of the big apartment buildings which lined the streets. Many of them, still integral in their essential structures, can be found scattered here and there around the city. Usually, they consisted of a rectangular

Vegetable vendor (marble from the III Century A.D.)

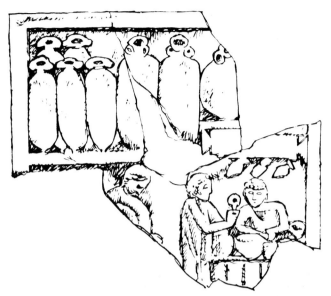

Beverage vendor shops (molded clay tablet)

Thermopolium (hypothetical reconstruction of the entrance)

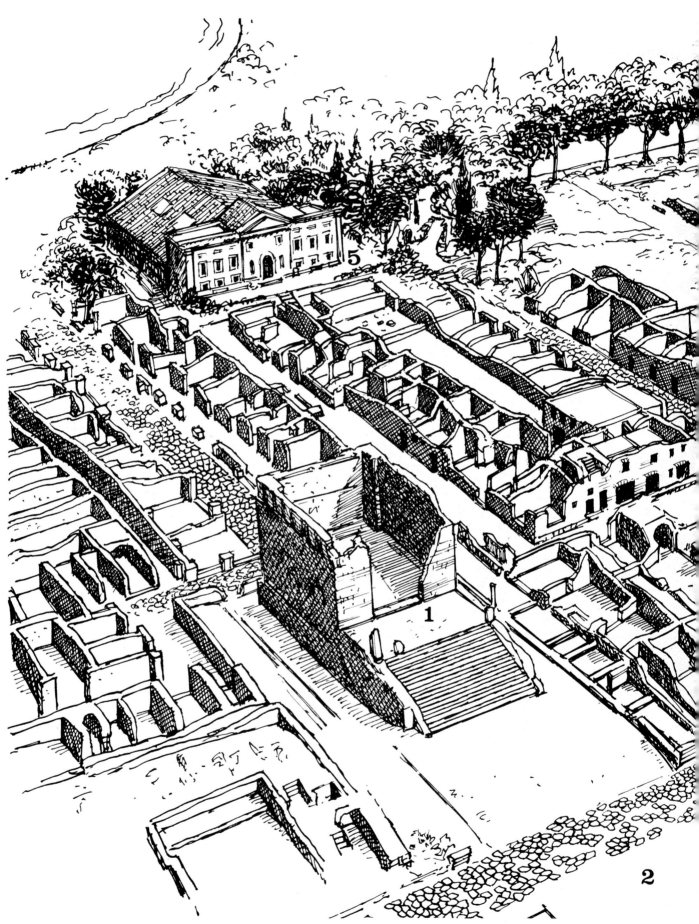

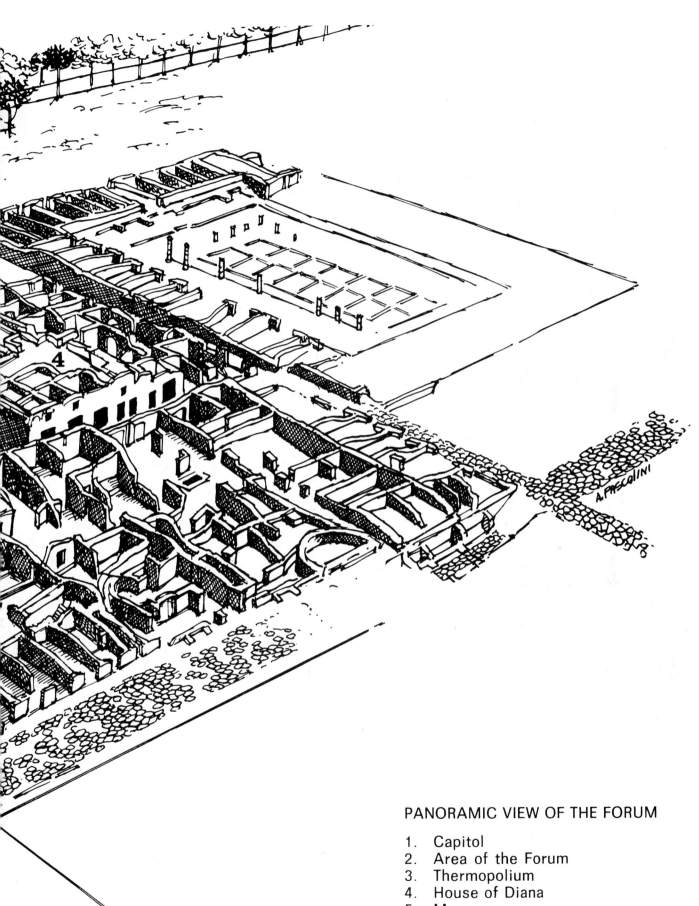

PANORAMIC VIEW OF THE FORUM

1. Capitol
2. Area of the Forum
3. Thermopolium
4. House of Diana
5. Museum

room. Near the entrance was a selling counter, often in brick. Shelves on the back walls held merchandise. In back of the shop, another room served as a storeroom for goods.

From time to time, in the back of these shops one can still notice a short brick staircase of three or four steps which ends in a small landing. From here, a wooden ladder led up to the mezzanine, a room created above the shop where in the majority of cases the shopkeepers lived.

### A LUXURIOUS PLACE

Among the shops along the streets were taverns and inns. Interesting are the Tavern of the Peacock and the Tavern of Alexander at the Marine Gate. Of particular interest on the street of the House of Diana is the «Thermopolium», a luxurious place which must have enjoyed a certain prestige in the city. Here, hot drinks and food were served. A comfortable and inviting back room permitted clients to linger in pleasant conversation.

### ARTISANS' SHOPS, LAUNDRIES AND DYE WORKS

In less representative premises were the artisans' shops where smiths, potters, saddlers, carpenters, etc., produced and sold their goods directly. Other, differently structured premises held dye works, tanner-

Molded clay tablet: smith's workshop (Isola Sacra)

Surgeon's sign (molded clay tablet)

62

Scene from a mill (molded clay tablet)

Bread baker (molded clay tablet)

Thermopolium (Counter Room)

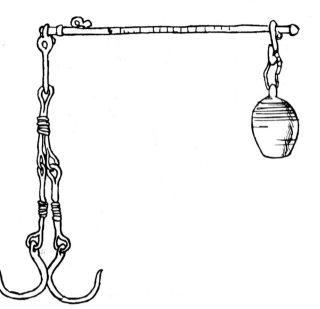

Steelyard

Water vendor (molded clay tablet)

ies, and laundries. A « fullonica » (laundry and dye works) still in excellent condition can be found on the Street of the Augustales. The « fullones » (the men in charge of this service) used to dye clothes in circular basins, still quite visible, by stamping them repeatedly with their feet.

*MILL, OVEN AND BREAD BAKERY*

At the intersection of the Street of the Mills and the Street of the House of Diana, there was a mill called Sylvanus's. There, the large millstones are still in place. On the floor's flagstones, even though they are now separated and out of place, it is possible to see hoof prints left by the donkeys that through centuries and centuries, with their continuous turning around the millstones, marked them indelibly. There probably was also an oven in the same apartment building where bread was baked. A shop on the Street of the House of Diana, communicating with the mill, makes one think that it was probably the bakery.

Bread baker (marble tablet)

Tavern scene (fragment of a sarcophagus)

Fullers

SOME EXAMPLES OF SHOPS *:

   9.  Tavern of the Peacock
 16.  Tavern of the Fishmongers
 28.  Tavern of Alexander Helix
 85.  Mill
 86.  Thermopolium
122.  Cleaner's

* The numbers correspond to those on the general map.

# THE TEMPLES AND PLACES OF WORSHIP

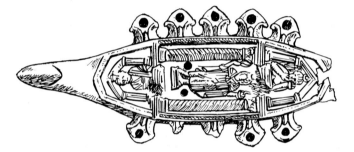

Oil lamp in the shape of a ship

*TEMPLES OF ROMAN DIVINITIES*

*TEMPLES OF ROMAN DIVINITIES*

The religious life in Ostia was from its very first centuries intense and manifold. Temples and places of worship arose throughout the city. Even though many of these temples have not come down to us, it has been possible to infer to whom they were dedicated from inscriptions found in the ruins. There were temples and shrines ded-

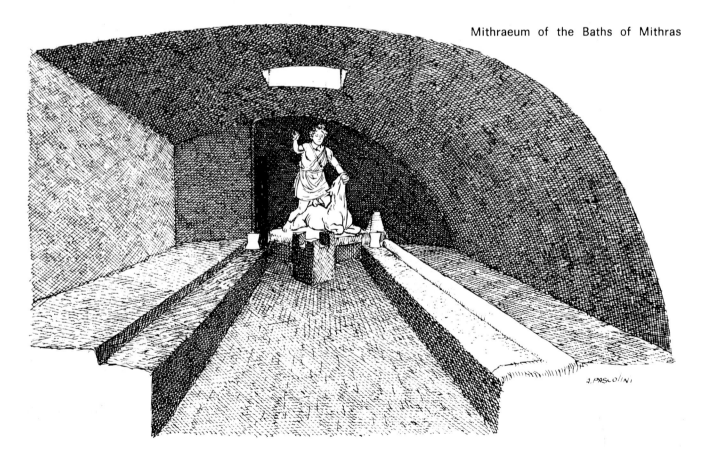

Mithraeum of the Baths of Mithras

A. PASCOLINI

Scene of a sacrifice (marble tablet)

The capitol

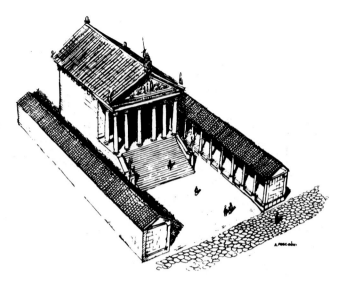

The capitol (hypothetical reconstruction)

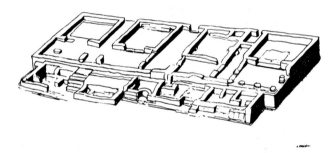

The four small temples (Republican age)

The four small temples (hypothetical reconstruction)

icated to Vulcanus, to the Capitol Triad (Jupiter, Juno, and Minerva), to Castor and Pollux, to Liber Pater (Father Bacchus), to Venus, to Fortune, to Ceres, to Hope, to Father Tiber, to « Genius » Colony of Ostia, to Hercules, to Sylvanus, to the Good Goddess, to Mars, to Neptune, to Apollo, to Diana, and to others. Moreover, the cults of emperors deified after their death, such as Trajan, Hadrian, Marcus Aurelius, and Septimius Severus, were very thriving.

### TEMPLES OF ORIENTAL DIVINITIES

Into Ostia, port of Rome, however, poured peoples from every corner of the Mediter-ranean basin for their commerce and it was normal, therefore, that they bring with them the uses and customs of their lands and that they build temples to their gods. This is evidenced by the shrines dedicated to Magna Mater (the Great Mother), to Attis, to Isis, to Serapis, to Mithras.

Sixteen, *mithraea*, places of worship dedicated to Mithras, scattered throughout the city testify to the great diffusion of this oriental religion. Among the most suggestive and strange is without doubt the *mithraeum* of the Baths of Mithras. This *mithraeum* was made out of one of the baths's unused underground cisterns and gets its light from a small trapdoor in its vault.

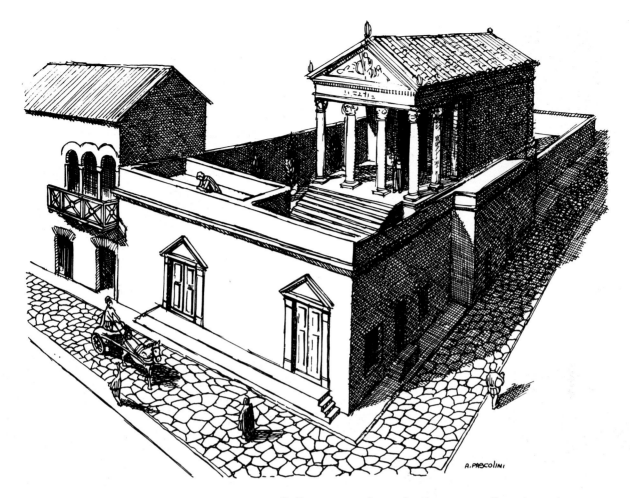

Collegiate temple on the Decumanus (hypothetical reconstruction)

## PRIVATE TEMPLES

Colleges, associations of persons of the same profession such as naval carpenters or masons, had their own private temples, and small votive chapels are found here and there in apartment buildings, artisans' shops, and baths.

## A HEBREW SYNAGOGUE AND CHRISTIAN BASILICA.

A Hebrew synagogue demonstrates that a fair size Jewish community lived in Ostia from the first century after Christ.

With the advent of Christianity, Ostia had its Christian martyrs such as the Virgin Aurea and in 313 A.D. there was a first Bishop of Ostia. Constantine built a Christian basilica. Monica, St. Augustine's mother, died here.

TEMPLES AND SHRINES OF PARTICULAR INTEREST *:

   3.  Shrine of Attis
  12.  Temple of Rome and Augustus
  63.  Temple of Hercules
  70.  Capitol
 117.  Collegiate Temple

   * The numbers correspond to those on the general map.

# THE FORICAE

A. PASCOLINI

In the large apartment buildings, in the thermae, in the public buildings, a room was always set aside as a public toilet; rarely has any been found in private homes or apartments. Exceptions to this rule are only a few late *domus* such as the *Domus* of the Fortuna Annonaria and the *Domus* of the Protiro.

Public toilet in the House of the Triclinums on the Street of the Public Toilet

Public toilets consisted of long marble benches with holes and could accomodate many persons at one time; nor did that create uneasiness. Double turnstyle doors such as those in the public toilet of the House of the Triclinums prevented passers-by from prying.

# THE HOUSES

Insula of the Muses (floor plan)

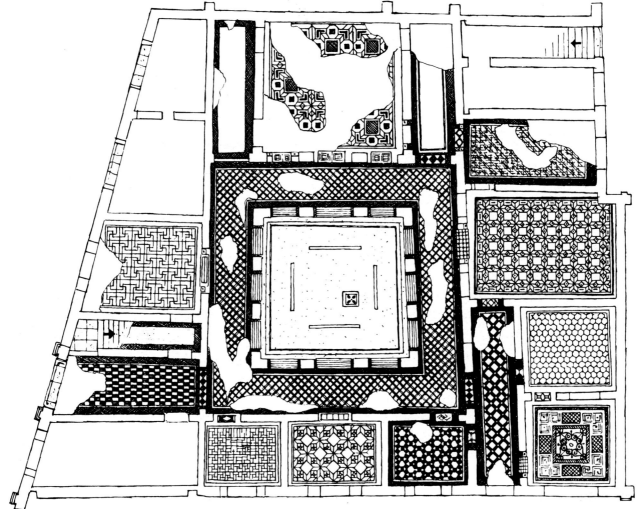

A. PASCOLINI

*DOMUS WITH ATRIUM AND PERISTYLE*

Ever since the Republican era, the ancient inhabitants of Ostia lived in brick houses. It is still possible to see traces of these constructions in the area of the old *castrum* next to the Capitol on the Street of the Republican Houses. These were structured

72

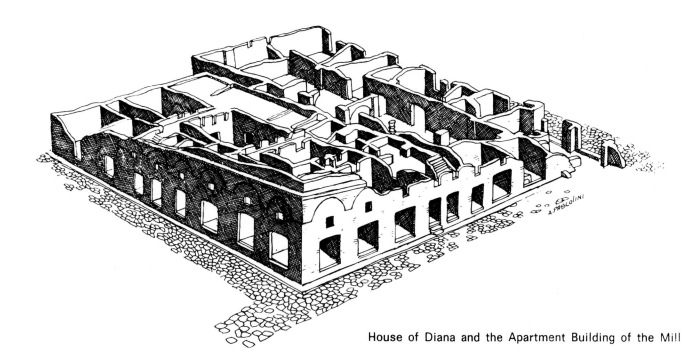

House of Diana and the Apartment Building of the Mill

**House of Diana and the Apartment Building of the Mill (hypothetical reconstruction)**

differently according to the social class of those who lived in them and went from the *domus* with its atrium and peristyle, generally one floor only, with its rooms surrounding a central open court from which they got air and light, to the mezzanines situated above the taverns where shopkeepers and common people lived.

Area of the forum

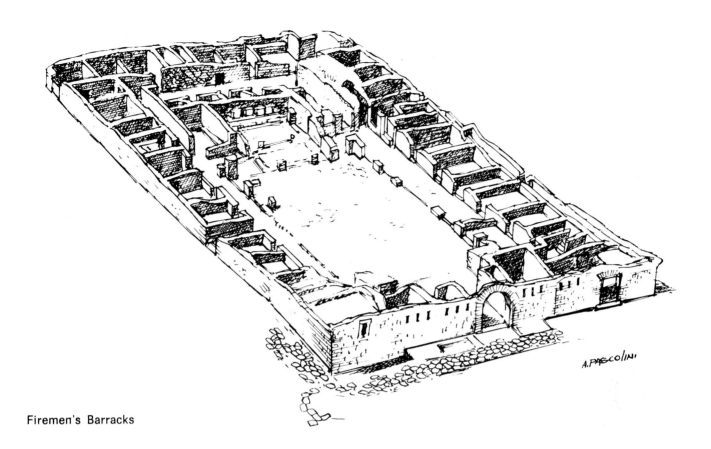

Firemen's Barracks

Firemen's Barracks (hypothetical reconstruction)

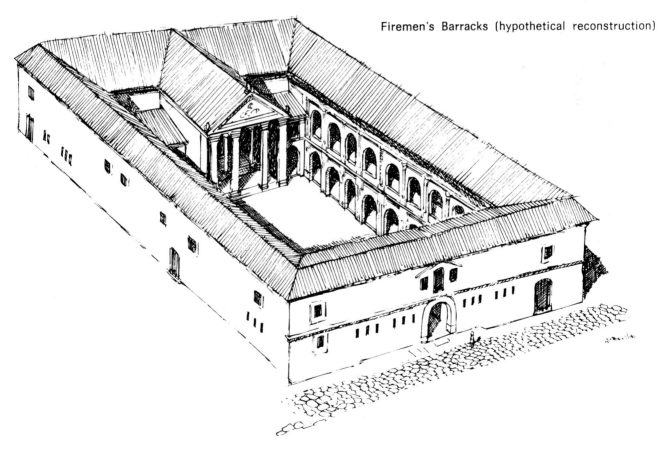

75

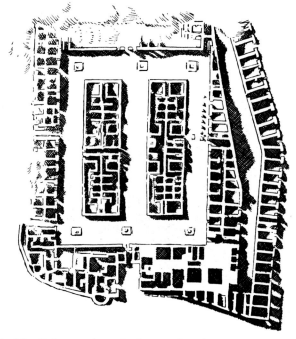

Residential complex of the garden homes

Domus of the Fish (floor plan)

A. PROCOLINI

But the real building development in Ostia took place during the Imperial period when entire blocks of apartment housing rose, divided into *insulae*. These reached three or four stories for a total height of over sixteen yards, so that already at that time confrontations arose over this form of building speculation and the Roman Senate, with rigorous laws, forbade their exceeding certain limits. These enormous apartment buildings were generally made up of stores on the ground floor and apartments on the above floors which in many cases were adorned by balconies. Inside of the building was a courtyard which allowed light to reach the rooms facing it.

*GARDEN HOMES OF THE RESIDENTIAL CENTER*

Of notable interest are the garden homes which reveal in their structure the idea of the residential center with apartments of considerable prestige which surround a square garden decorated with six large fountains.

Interesting for the richness of their paintings and for their mosaics, still sufficiently preserved, are several houses.

| 36. | Domus of the Dioscuri |
|---|---|
| 38. | Insula of the Yellow Walls |
| 40. | Insula of the Muses |
| 41. | Insula of the Painted Vaults |
| 62. | Domus of Cupid and Psyche |
| 128. | Domus of the Fortuna Annonaria |
| E. | Domus of the Fish |

* The numbers correspond to those on the general map.

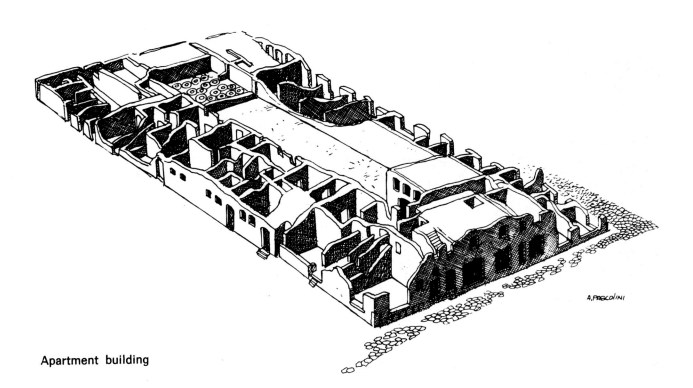

Apartment building

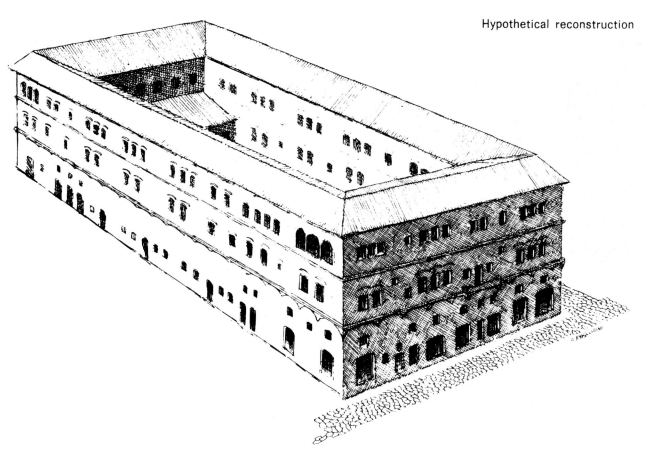

Hypothetical reconstruction

77

A.PASCOLINI

Insula of the Muses (some frescoes from a room)

R. PASCOLINI

# THE MOSAICS

**BRICK FLOORS, INLAYS AND MOSAICS**

Mosaic flooring deserves a separate mention. Thousands and thousands of square yards of mosaic floors still emerge from the ruins of Ostia. Fortunately neglected by material seekers who drew from these ruins throughout the various centuries because of their impracticable re-use, they have come down to us almost in their entirety.

Ever since the early Republican period, the houses of Ostia were decorated with

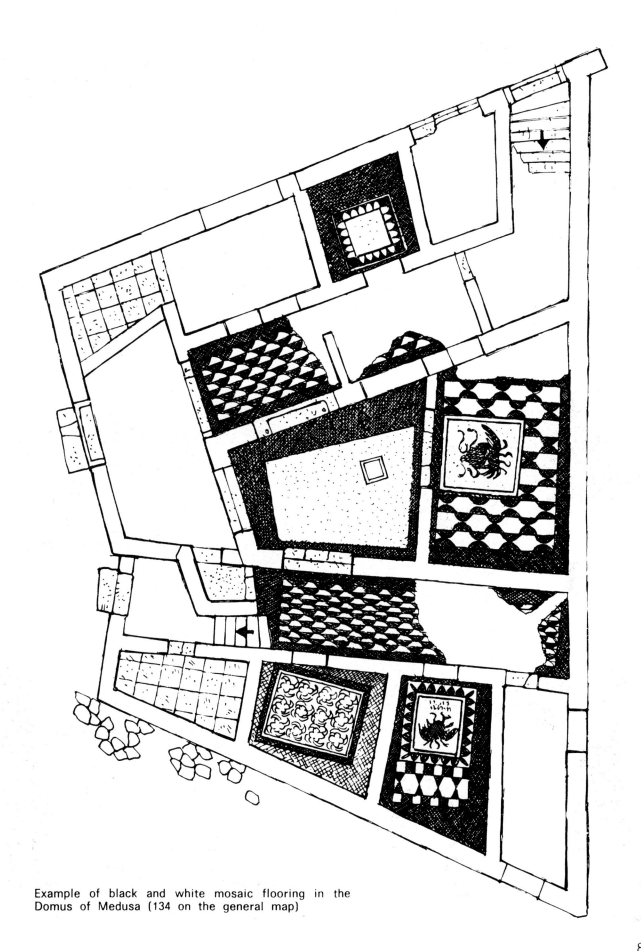

Example of black and white mosaic flooring in the
Domus of Medusa (134 on the general map)

mosaic floors; this kind of flooring mixed with lime was at that time very simple and schematic and was usually laid in the richest rooms of the house. Secondary rooms or corridors were paved with bricks or with a mixture of lime and bits of crockery today called « coccio pesto » (pounded bricks).

Ostia's mosaics were made up with small quadrangular pieces, about a quarter of an inch each side, almost always in black and white.

The mosaic's major development, however, was during the Imperial period when almost all rooms were paved with this technique. In the richest *domus* and in the temples, mosaics sometimes were alternated with rare marble inlays (*opus sectile*); an excellent example of *opus sectile* can be admired in the city's museum, recently restructured under the guidance of the Superintendent Santa Maria Scrinari Valnea.

### GEOMETRIC FORMS AND FIGURES

While in the *domus* the mosaic was used to shape more or less elaborate geometric forms, in the thermae the figure prevailed. Tritons, mythical marine figures half fish and half man, or Nereids, sea nymphs, wander among fish, ships, and lighthouses. Scenes of gladiators fighting or other kinds of figures were constantly repeated from room to room.

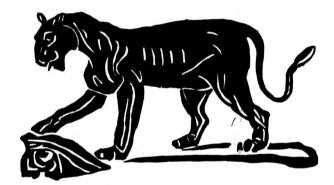

But mosaics were not used only for baths or temples or *domus*; it is possible to find them in stores as well with symbolic representations and publicity inscriptions (a clear example of this is the Corporations' Forum) or in outdoor gymnasiums as in the Baths of the Forum. Its maximum use was had in the Baths of the Seven Sages where a delicate decoration in colored mosaic made of vitreous paste even adorned the walls of the cupola- covered circular room.

During the late Empire, mosaics in large pieces, about one and a half inches each side, were commonly used for secondary rooms such as courtyards, arcades, and corridors.

A. PASCCLINI

# THE PAINTINGS AND GRAFFITI

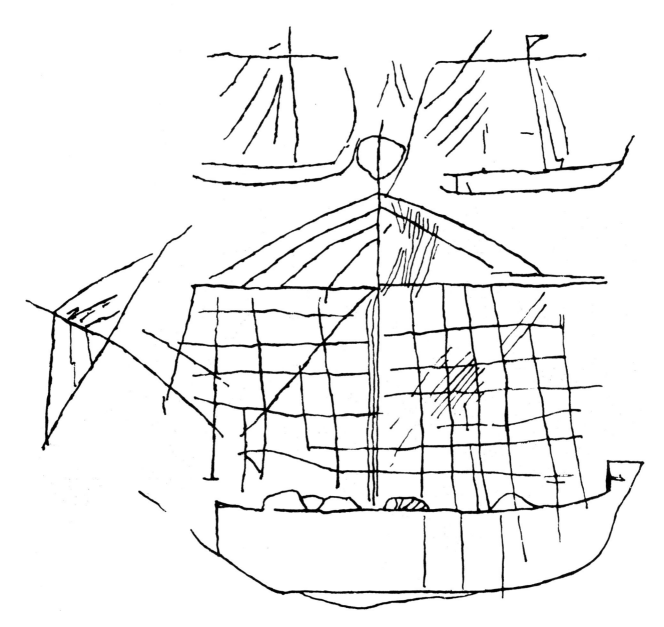

## DETERIORATED FRESCOES

Abandoned little by little as the disorganization increased (between the VI and VII Century A.D.), Ostia underwent the consequences of it with ruinous falling of its buildings; many of the pictorial decorations which adorned the walls, painted with the fresco technique, deteriorated rapidly once exposed to the harsh weather. The brilliant Pompeian reds, the dark Sienna browns, the deep turquoise blues paled, fading forever into calcined grayish-brown spots.

# DIE BEKEHRTE
## (The Converted One)

Johann Wolfgang von Goethe

Max Stange

Andantino.

Bei dem Glanz der A - bend - rö - the ging__ ich still den
As I roam'd the woods at lei - sure In__ the eve - ning

Wald__ ent - lang,          Da - mon sass und
hour__ so still,          Da - mon sat and

blies__ die Flö - te, dass es von__ den Fel - sen klang:
piped__ for plea - sure, E - cho an - swer'd from the hill:

so la_____ re
so la_____ re

Und er zog mich zu\_ sich nie - der, küss - te mich so
Then the swain, my steps de - lay - ing, Kissed me soft - ly,

hold und süss.\_\_\_
looked and sighed.\_\_\_

14

Und— ich sag-te, bla - se wie - der, und der gu - te Jun - ge blies: so
But— I bade him still— be play - ing, And the kind - ly youth complied: so

la_____ re la_____ la
la_____ re la_____ la

la_____ la la.
la_____ la la.

Mei - ne Ruh' ist nun ver - lo - ren, mei - ne
Now, a - las, I wan - der lone - ly, All___ my

Freu - de floh da - von, und__ ich hör' vor mei - nen
joy is turn'd to pain; Dream - ing, wak - ing, hear__ I

Oh - ren im - mer nur den al - ten Ton:
on - ly Da - mon's sweet and ten - der strain:

so la__ re la__
so la__ re la__

la la__ la la.__
la la__ la la.__

# DER BLUMENSTRAUSS
## (The Nosegay)

Felix Mendelssohn

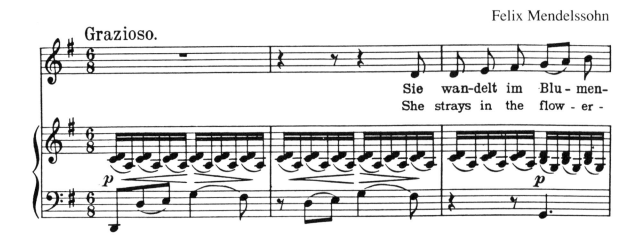

Sie wan-delt im Blu-men-gar - ten und mu-stert den bun - ten Flor,_____ und
She strays in the flow-er-gar - den, Sur-vey-ing the gau - dy scene,_____ While

al - le die Klei - nen war - ten und schau-en zu ihr em-
all the wee flow-ers are wait - - ing, And gaz-ing on her, their

por. „Und seid ihr denn Früh - lings-bo - - ten, ver -
queen. "And are ye the her-alds of Spring - -tide, Fore-

kün - dend was stets so neu,_____ so wer-det auch mei - ne
tell - ing the ev - er - new,_____ Then bear me a mes-sage of

Bo - ten an ihn, der mich liebt so treu, an
Spring-tide To him who loves me true to

ihn,_____ der mich liebt _____ so
him _____ who loves _____ me

treu."
true."

18

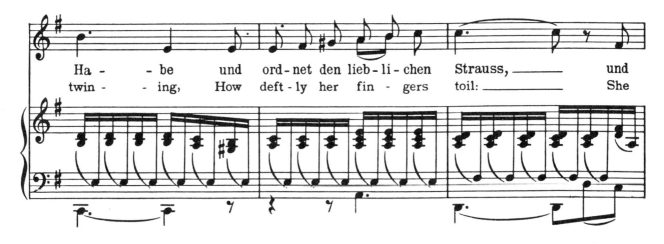

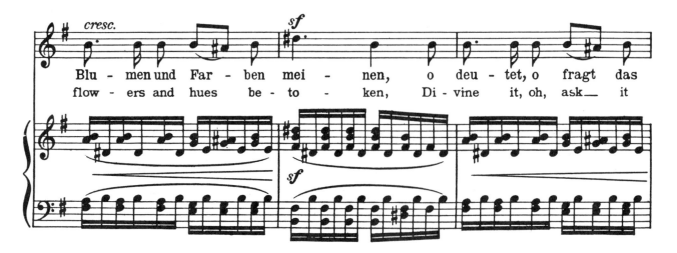

nicht, \_\_\_\_\_ wenn aus den Au-gen der Ei - nen der sü - sse - ste Früh-ling
not, \_\_\_\_\_ When Spring so sweet-ly hath spo - ken In looks that with love are

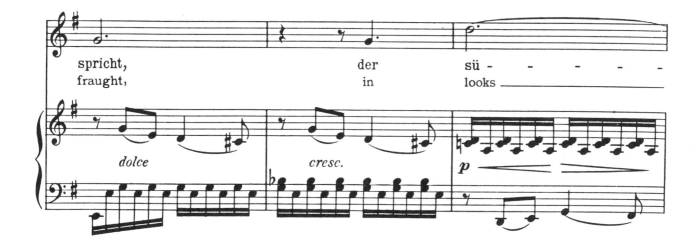

spricht, der sü - - - -
fraught, in looks _____

- - -sse-ste Früh - - ling spricht.
that with love _____ are fraught!

# THE CHERRY TREE

Margaret Rose

Armstrong Gibbs

Time of performance 2—2¼ mins.

The sad, sweet birds of the Spring -

time are sing - ing a - gain to me. ____

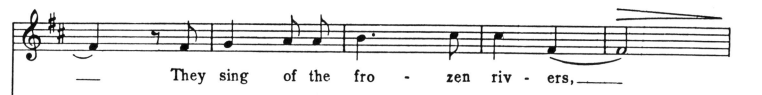

They sing of the fro - zen riv - ers, ____

Pi - ping soft and low _____ Till I

think I hear_____ your foot - steps danc - ing

poco rit. *a tempo*

a - cross the snow.

poco rit. *mp a tempo*

Sing, birds! Sing songs of the

Spring - time, Sing high

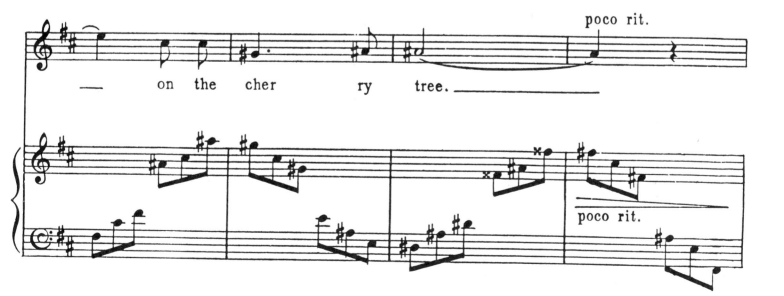

— on the cher ry tree.

Sing of my love in the North - land ——— As my love once

sang to me. ——————

Hush, birds! the cher-ry in si - lence Is

let - ting her pet - als fall _____ For

one whose danc - ing foot - steps Will nev - er

come _____ at all. _____

# CHI VUOL LA ZINGARELLA

Giovanni Paisiello

so bene in-do -vi - nar.
Their fortune I can tell;
I giovani al can -to - ne
The laddies at the inn,— too,

so meglio stuzzi - car. A— vecchi in-na -mo -ra -ti scal - dar fo le cer-
I can amuse as well. When old men feel love burning, I— set their heads a-

vel -la, scal - dar fo— le cer-vel -la, a— vecchi inna -mo -ra - ti. Chi
turning, I— set their heads a - turn-ing, When old men feel love burn - ing. Who'll

vuol la zin-ga - rel -la, chi vuol la zin-ga -rel -la? Si - gnori, ec -co-la—
try the Gip-sy pretty, Who'll try the Gip-sy pretty? Come one and all to—

qua, si - gnori, ec - co - la__ qua.
me, come one and all__ to__ me.

Le don-ne sul bal -
For ladies at their

co - ne so bene in-do-vi - nar.
win - dow Their fortune I can tell,

I giovani al can-
The laddies at the

to - ne so meglio stuzzi - car. A vecchi in-na-mo -
inn, too, I can amuse as well. When old men feel love

ra - ti, a vecchi in-na-mo-ra - ti scal-dar fo__ le cer-vel-la. Chi
burn - ing I set their heads a - turn-ing, I__ set their heads a-turning. Who'll

vuol la zin - ga - rel - la gra - zio - sa, ac - cor - ta e
try the Gip - sy pret - ty, So win - ning, wise and

bel - la? Si - gno - ri, ec - co - la___ qua;___ si -
wit - ty, As___ one and___ all may___ see,___ as

gno - ri, ec - co - la___ qua, gra - zi - o - sa, ac - cor - ta e
one___ and___ all__ may___ see; So___ win - ning, wise and

bel - la, gra - zi - o - sa, accor - ta e bel - la. Si - gno - ri, ec - co - la
wit - ty, so___ winning, wise and wit - ty, As one and all may

qua,   gra - zi - o - sa, ac - cor - ta e   bel - la,   gra - zi - o - sa, ac - cor - ta e
see,   so__ winning  and  so   wit - ty,   so__ winning, wise and

*animando sempre e cresc.*

bel - la,   Si - gno - ri, ec - co - la   qua,   si - gno - ri,   si -
wit - ty,   As  one  and  all may   see,   so winning,   so

gno - ri,   si - gno - ri, ec - co - la   qua,   si - gno - ri,   si -
wit - ty,   As  one  and  all may   see?   so win - ning,   so

*rit.*

gnori,   si - gnori, ec - co - la  qua.
wit - ty,  Come one and  all  to  me.

# CLOUD-SHADOWS

Katharine Pyle

James H. Rogers

**Slowly and dreamily**

I wish I could ride on the shad-ows of clouds That drift a-cross the

hill; O-ver the mead-ow and out of sight They sweep so smooth and still.

O-ver the dai - sy field they passed, And not a dai - sy stirr'd; They

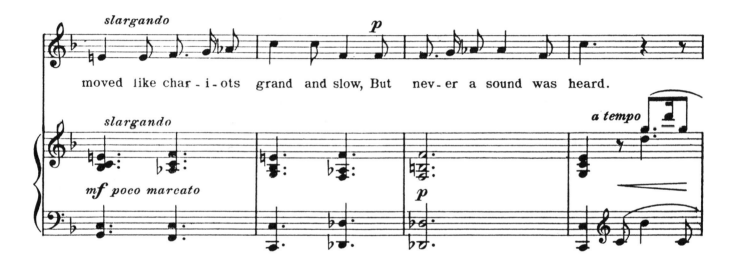

moved like char-i-ots grand and slow, But nev-er a sound was heard.

wish I could ride on the shad-ows of clouds, Could ride till, the jour - ney done,      I'd

find my-self at the      end of the world, Where the earth and the sky are  one.

# CHRISTOPHER ROBIN IS SAYING HIS PRAYERS
## (Vespers)

A. A. Milne

H. Fraser-Simson

cold's so cold, And the hot's so hot. Oh! God bless Dad - dy I

*Slower again*

quite for - got. If I o - pen my fin - gers a lit - tle bit more, I can

*Quickening*

see Nan - ny's dress - ing gown on the door. It's a beau - ti - ful blue, but it

has - n't a hood. Oh! God bless Nan - ny and make _ her good. ____

*Slower*

*Again quickening*

Mine has a hood and I lie in bed And pull the hood right

o - ver my head. And I shut my eyes and I curl up small, And

no-bod - y knows that I'm there at all. Oh! Thank you God, for a love - ly day, And

*A little slower*

*Quickening*

what was the oth - er I had to say? I said "Bless Dad - dy" so

what can it be? Oh! Now I re-mem-ber it, God— bless me.

*Sleepy again*

Lit - tle boy kneels at the foot of the bed, Droops on the lit - tle hands

*More and more sleepily*

lit - tle gold head, Hush! Hush! Whis - per who dares!

*Out on tip-toe, he's asleep*

Chris - to - pher Rob - in is say-ing his prayers.—

# CRABBED AGE AND YOUTH

William Shakespeare

Maude Valérie White

Con spirito.

Youth like sum-mer morn,.... Age.. like win-ter wea-ther,

Youth................. like sum-mer brave, Age... like win-ter

molto *rit.*

bare.

Youth is full of plea-sure, Age is full of care;

Youth is full of sport, Age's breath is short;

# CRUCIFIXION

African American spiritual
arranged by John Payne

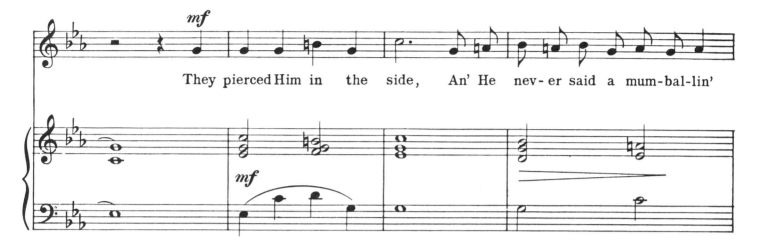

They pierced Him in the side, An' He nev-er said a mum-bal-lin'

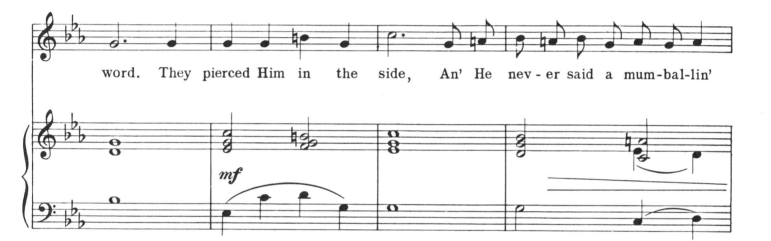

word. They pierced Him in the side, An' He nev-er said a mum-bal-lin'

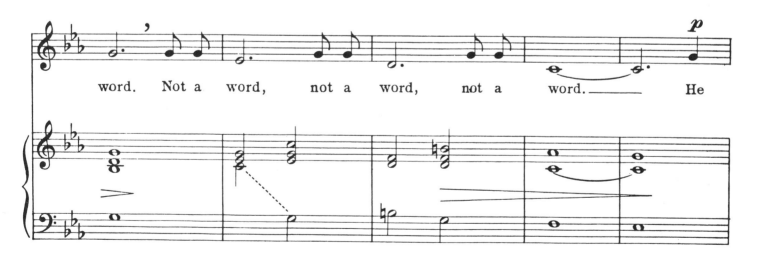

word. Not a word, not a word, not a word._____ He

now    Is    hung    with    bloom    a  -  long    the

bough,_____    And    stands_____    a - bout    the    wood  -  land

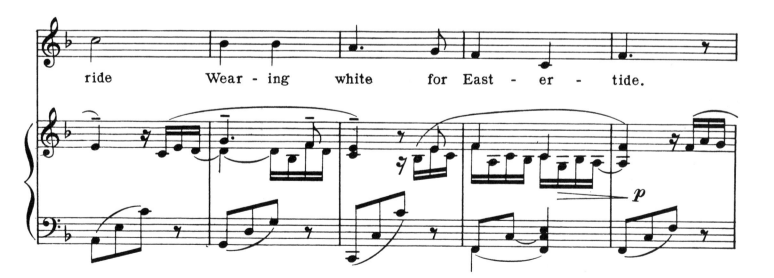

ride    Wear - ing    white    for    East - er - tide.

Now, of my three - score years and ten.

Twen - ty will not come a - gain,

And take from sev - en - ty springs a

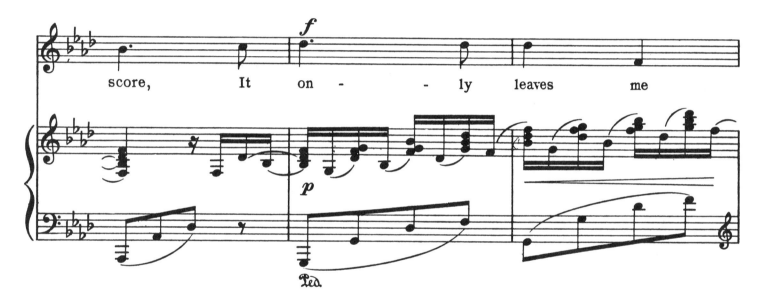

score, It on - ly leaves me

fif - ty more.

And since to look at things in bloom

*tranquillo e sempre pp*

Ped. ✻

Fif - ty springs are lit - tle room,

A - bout the wood - lands I will go To

pp

mp

see the cher - ry hung_____ with

snow._____

# MORNING

from the "Atlanta Constitution"
by Frank L. Stanton

Oley Speaks

*From the "Atlanta Constitution;" used by permission.

*Copyright, 1931, by G. Schirmer, Inc.*

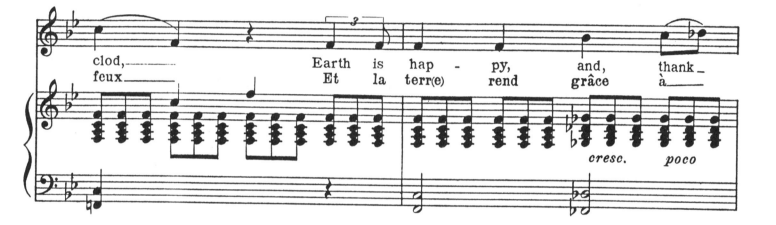

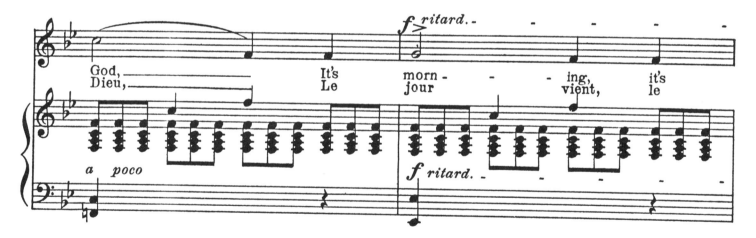

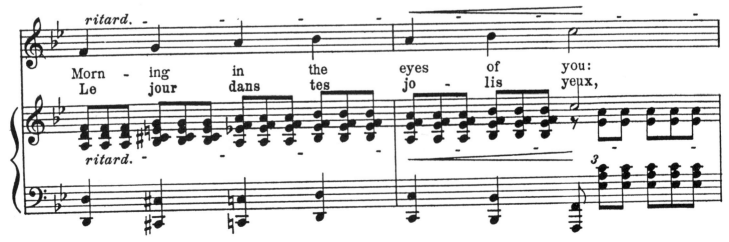

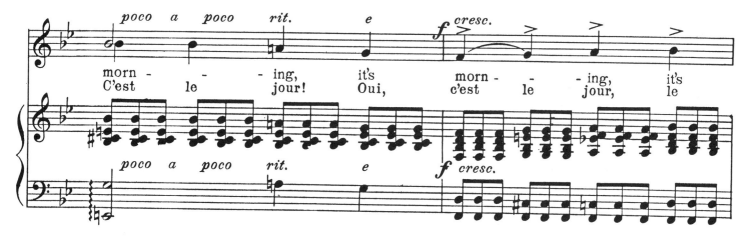

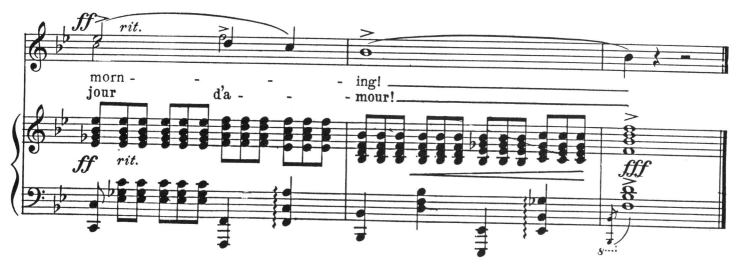

# PRAYER

Hermann Hagedorn

David W. Guion

Not blind - ly, not in ha - tred, Lord, let me do my

part; Keep o - pen, oh, keep o - pen, dear Lord,—

My eyes, my mind, my heart!—

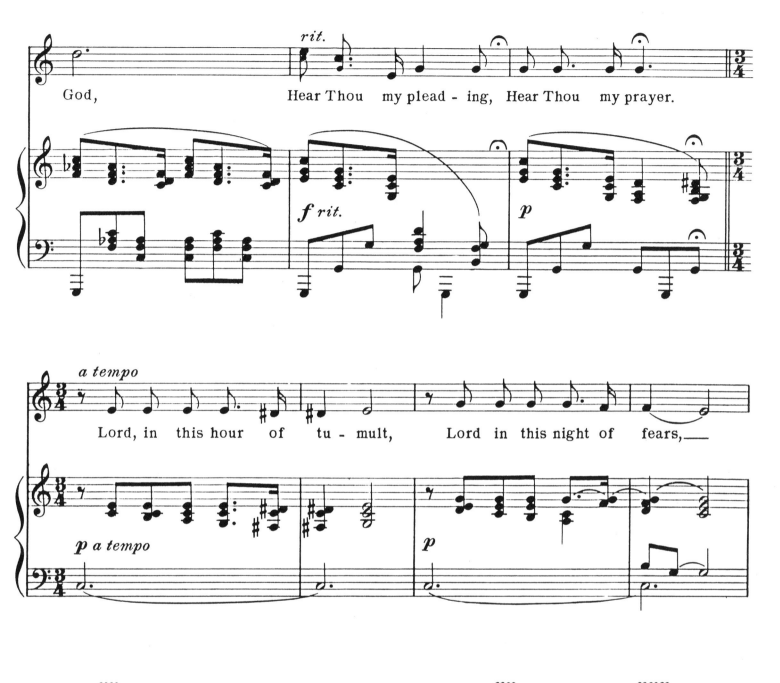

God,    Hear Thou my plead - ing, Hear Thou    my prayer.

Lord, in this hour of tu - mult,    Lord in this night of    fears,___

Keep o - pen, oh, keep o - pen    My eyes,    my ears.

# PREGÚNTALE A LAS ESTRELLAS

Latin American folksong
arranged by Edward Kilenyi

_Moderato._

Pre-Go

-gún-tale á las es-tre-llas, si no de no-che me ven llo-rar, Pre-
_ask of the high stars gleam-ing, If my tears fall not through-out the night._ Go

-gún-ta-les si no bus-co, pa-ra a-do-rar-te la so-le-dad. Pre-
_ask if I seek not dream-ing, For thee till the dawn brings light._ Go

-gun-tale al man-so ri-o, si el llan-to mi-o no vé co-rrer, Pre-
_ask of the murm'-ring stream-let, If my pale sha-dow-y form goes by._ Go

_cresc._  _f_

-gún-tale á to-do el mun - do si no es pro-fun-do mi pa - de - cer.
*ask of all cre - a - tion If thou art not, love, my soul's one cry.*

*colla voce*

Ya nun-ca du - des que yo te quie - ro, Que por tí
*Ah! doubt not dear - est, that I a - dore thee, For thee I*

*mf*

*colla voce*

mue - ro, lo - co de a - mor; A na-die a - mas, á na-die
*per - ish dis-traught with love; Thou lov-est no one, Thy heart beats*

*colla voce*

*P*

*cresc.*

quie - res, O - ye las que-jas, o - ye las que-jas de mi a - mor.
*cold - ly, Oh! hear the plead-ing, Oh! hear the plead-ing of my fond love.*

*f*

Pre -
*Go*

-gún-ta-le á las flo-res, si mis a - mo-res les cuen-to yo, Cuan-
*ask of the sweet flowers bloom-ing If of my sor-rows I told not all. Go*

-do la ca-lla - da no-che cie-rra su bro-che, su-spi - ro yo, Pre-
*ask of the wild birds sing-ing If I sigh when the night doth fall. Go*

-gún-ta-le á las a - ves, si tu no sa-bes lo que es a - mor, Pre-
*ask of the dew - y mea-dows If thy love holds not my heart in thrall. Go*

# O REST IN THE LORD
## from *Elijah*

Psalm 37

Felix Mendelssohn

sires,___ and He shall give thee thy heart's de - sires. Com-mit thy way un-

to Him,___ and trust in Him; com-mit thy way un - to Him,___ and trust in

Him, and fret_ not thy - self___ be-cause of e - vil do - ers. O rest in the

Lord, wait pa-tient-ly for Him, wait pa-tient-ly for Him; O rest in the

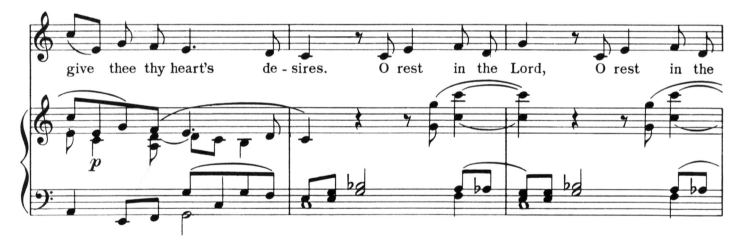

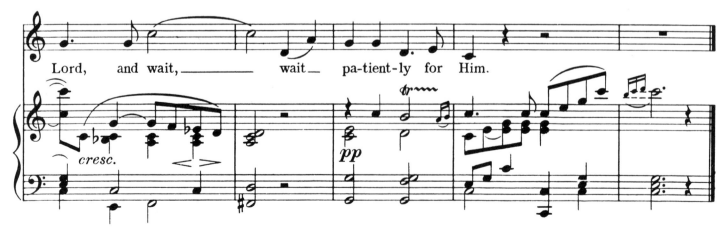

# OH SLEEP, WHY DOST THOU LEAVE ME?

## from *Semele*

William Congreve

George Frideric Handel

*The Editor's piano accompaniment is founded on Handel's unfigured bass.

Oh _____ sleep, oh_ sleep, oh sleep, a-gain de-ceive me, oh

sleep, a-gain de-ceive me, to my arms re - store my_ wan - d'ring

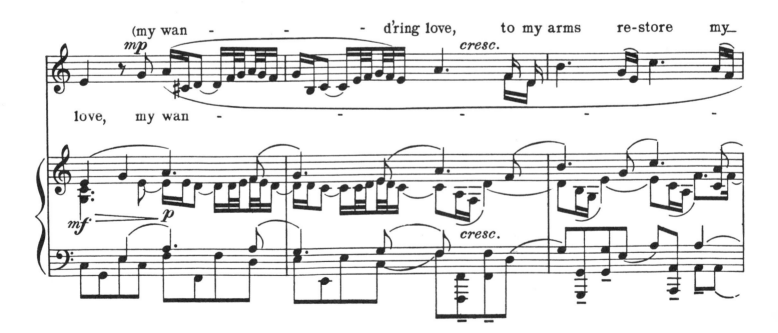

(my wan - - - d'ring love, to my arms re-store my_

love, my wan - - - - - -